Walk Ha‹
The Cha‛

CW00664060

AN
ESSENTIAL GUIDE TO
HELP YOU COMPLETE
HADRIAN'S WALL WALK

BRIAN SMAILES

Walk Guides   **THE YORKSHIRE DALES TOP TEN**
ISBN 978-0-9526900-5-4

THE DERBYSHIRE TOP TEN
ISBN 978-1-903568-03-3

THE COMPLETE ISLE OF WIGHT COASTAL FOOTPATH
ISBN 978-0-9526900-6-1

ISLE OF WIGHT, NORTH TO SOUTH – EAST TO WEST
ISBN 978-1-903568-07-1

THE SCOTTISH COAST TO COAST WALK
ISBN 978-0-9526900-8-5

THE YORKSHIRE 3 PEAKS WALK
ISBN 978-1-903568-46-0

THE YORKSHIRE 3 PEAKS WALK SKETCH MAP & ROUTE GUIDE
ISBN 978-1-903568-23-1

17 WALKS IN GLEN NEVIS
ISBN 978-1-903568-05-7

THE GREAT GLEN WAY
ISBN 978-1-903568-13-2

THE LANCASHIRE TRAIL
ISBN 978-1-903568-10-1

THE LYKE WAKE WALK GUIDE
ISBN 978-1-903568-47-7

THE 1066 COUNTRY WALK
ISBN 978-1-903568-00-2

THE NATIONAL 3 PEAKS WALK
ISBN 978 1-903568-24-8

SHORT WALKS IN THE LAKE DISTRICT
ISBN 978-1-903568-20-0

JOHN O'GROATS TO LANDS END
ISBN 978-1-903568-18-7

Tourist Guides **TOURIST GUIDE TO VARADERO, CUBA**
ISBN 978-1-903568-08-8

EXPLORE – FORT WILLIAM & GLEN NEVIS
ISBN 978-1-903568-25-5

Obtainable from bookshops or direct from the address below. See web site for book details. www.chall-pub.co.uk

Walk Hadrian's Wall

ISBN 978-1-903568-40-8

First Edition 2007

CHALLENGE PUBLICATIONS
7, EARLSMERE DRIVE, BARNSLEY. S71 5HH

Brian Smailes

Holds the record for the fastest 4 and 5 continuous crossings of the Lyke Wake Walk over the North York Moors. He completed the 210 miles over rough terrain on 5 crossings in June 1995 taking 85 hours and 50 minutes. In 2006 he completed his 50th crossing.

His most recent venture was to walk the Inca Trail in Peru in 2005, visiting Lake Titticacca and Bolivia while in the area. In August 2003 he walked from John O'Groats to Lands End, compleing it in 34 days. In August 2001 he cycled from Lands End to John O`Groats, a journey of over 900 miles in 6 days 13 hours 18 minutes. This involved carrying food, clothing and tent, and was completed without support between both ends.

Brian lectures on outdoor pursuit courses and between these travels extensively on walking expeditions and projects around Great Britain and abroad. A further expedition to China is imminent in March 2007.

Long distance running, canoeing and sub aqua diving are other sports he enjoys, completing 25 marathons and canoeing the Caledonian Canal 3 times. Brian has dived all around the UK coastline as well as Thailand, Cuba and Mexico.

Having travelled extensively throughout the UK, Europe, Caribbean and South America, Brian has recently been writing international travel guides to enable the holidaymaker to access the world with ease and enjoy it as much as he does.

ACKNOWLEDGEMENTS

It is with thanks to the following people for assistance, that this book has been published: -

Chris Barber for accompanying me on the walk.
Pam Smailes
Photographs - Brian Smailes, Chris Barber

Brian Smailes is identified as author of this book in accordance with Copyright Act 1988.

No part of this publication may be reproduced by any means without prior permission in writing from the publisher.

First Published 2007
ISBN 978-1-903568-40-8

Published by Challenge Publications, 7, Earlsmere Drive, Ardsley, Barnsley, S71 5HH.
www.chall-pub.co.uk

Printed by Dearne Valley Printers, Wath upon Dearne, Rotherham.

The information recorded in this book is believed by the author to be correct at time of publication. No liabilities can be accepted for any inaccuracies found. Anyone using this guide should refer to their map in conjunction with this book. The description or representation of a route used is not evidence of a right of way.

CONTENTS

PHOTOGRAPHS

PREFACE TO THE 1st EDITION

It gives me great pleasure to present this 1st edition of Walk Hadrian's Wall. Hadrian's Wall runs 84 miles from west to east, starting at Bowness-on-Solway (Maia), and finishing at Wallsend (Segedunum). It has been a world heritage site since 1987 and is referred to as 'the most complex and best preserved of the frontiers of the Roman Empire!

Why walk west to east? The prevailing wind often blows across the country so walking with your back to the wind may help a little. You may find it easier to walk from Bowness-on-Solway, as within a few hours you enter Carlisle, a large city where you can buy supplies or tend to any ailments if necessary before tackling the more challenging central section. Another reason is that if walking from Wallsend, once out of the built up area, if you have a problem then you do not pass through any other towns where you may be able to get supplies/advice for quite a distance.

Hadrian's Wall consists of 84 miles of wall, path and track, 80 mile castles and 15 forts spread along the route of the wall. The wall appears then disappears throughout the route. Parts have been dismantled, build over or grassed over. Other parts are well preserved.

Throughout the route there is excellent scenery and stunning views of the wall and surrounding countryside. There are 'wall' signposts, usually with an acorn sign on them to signify a national trail, and the route is generally well marked.

There are campsites on route, but not many, and sometimes a fair distance apart. Equally B&B's are not always where you want them to be, so research the route before you go and book ahead if possible, especially during peak holiday times.

Throughout the route, there are café's and public houses, many are mentioned in this book and most of them have food, which makes life easier.

This book is a guide to the route and the O.S. maps recommended at the back of this book should be used. The facts and figures, heights, walk times and distances are included so you have all the necessary information you need to complete this walk.

Should you wish to have further information about detailed places on route like forts or other historical places then I recommend contacting one of the T.I.C's listed at the back of this book for the appropriate leaflets.

Finally, a passport is available for those who wish to have a souvenir of their journey. You can get it free before you go and have it stamped on route at various places listed on the passport. When you have completed the walk, you can then purchase a certificate and badge (price in 2006 £2.95).

Contact T.I.Cs. in the area for further information. If you request an information pack via the website or email for one then a passport will be sent free with other general information covering the walk. See useful addresses/Hadrian's Wall Tourism at the back of this book.

Following the advice given in this book should enable all walkers to complete Hadrian's Wall Walk in a safe and competent manner.

Brian Smailes

SHORT HISTORY OF THE WALL

Hadrian's Wall was build as its name suggests by the Emperor Hadrian. The wall was built to mark the northern most boundary of Roman Britain. Between the sections are milecastles and turrets as well as forts, which housed the soldiers.

Initially a 'Stanegate' or fortified road was established along the Tyne. There were forts at Carlisle, Nether Denton, Vindolanda and Corbridge. The Stanegate and the forts served the Romans well but gradually there was an increase in trouble between those in the north and tribes in the south.

Hadrian visited the area in AD122 and it was then that the order was given for the wall to be built. The wall was to run between Wallsend and Bowness-on-Solway. It took 8 years to build and some 9000 workers to build it, as well as 3 legions of soldiers. It had 80 milecastles, i.e. one for every Roman mile. A Roman mile is 1620 yards so this doesn't actually add up.

A milecastle is a fortified gateway to allow people through. They usually housed approximately 12 soldiers. On the west side, some milecastles and parts of the wall were originally built of turf, as there was a shortage of stone.

Between the milecastles there were usually two turrets, and they were all built of stone. Turrets were really an observation tower and they provided shelter for the soldiers.

A Roman legion consisted of 5000 soldiers, which were divided into 10 cohorts of 100 men. Each legion also had 60 centurions and a senior centurion. This was the fighting machine they called the Roman army!

Hadrian died in AD138 and the wall was abandoned as his successor ventured further into Scotland, but 25 years later it was reused and refurbished. It continued to be used until AD411 when the Romans left our shores.

ROMAN FORTS ON ROUTE

These were the forts believed to be in existence during Hadrian's reign. Between these forts there were milecastles with 2 turrets between them. The wall itself was believed to be around 12 to 15 feet in height.

Bowness	*Maia*
Drumburgh	*Congavata*
Burgh by Sands	*Aballava*
Stanwix	*Uxelodunum*
Castlesteads	*Camboglanna*
Birdoswald	*Banna*
Great Chesters	*Aesica*
Housesteads	*Vercovicium*
Carrawburgh	*Brocolitia*
Chesters	*Cilurnum*
Halton Chesters	*Onnum*
Rudchester	*Vindobala*
Benwell	*Condercum*
Newcastle	*Pons Aelius*
Wallsend	*Segedunum*

Other forts numbering 32 altogether including the above existed as far down as Ravenglass on the west coast and South Shields on the east coast. In addition to the forts, there were temples, bridges, turrets, milecastles, cemeteries and civil settlements.

There is a wealth of information to get, places to see and things to do. Whatever your preferred activity or mode of travel, there is something for everyone along the wall or in the surrounding area.

THE VALLUM

The vallum is an area of around 40 metres wide, which included the wall, a fighting ditch, the Roman road or military way and two mounds. It was used as an area of defence.

On the northern side is the fighting ditch and near it the wall. This was believed to be around 12 - 15 feet in height. On the inside of the wall or the south side is the road, to enable the Roman army to move quickly along by the wall to wherever they were needed.

Then there were the mounds and ditch in between. These were to protect the soldiers and provide some defence between themselves and any tribe who may attack them from the English side. The Roman soldiers were between the devil and the deep blue sea! This was because they were liable to be attacked from either side

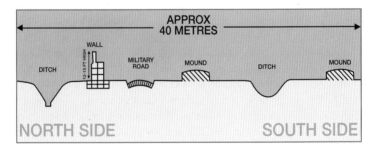

A Vallum
Sketch 13

THE CHALLENGE
Route Synopsis

The route between Bowness-on-Solway to Wallsend, although only 84 miles is a tough challenge. It initially starts with some virtually flat walking, but as you walk towards the central and Pennines section, it becomes more undulating. The best scenery is in the central section.

The whole route is a very enjoyable walk with different scenery over each crag and hillside. The initial stages take you along roads, over fields and through villages. There are not always grass paths to walk along but there are plenty of signposts with a white acorn on them, which denotes a National Trail, which keep you on the designated route.

Arriving at Carlisle, you are not far from the city centre and any food, accommodation or other items that are wanted can be purchased here. Leaving Carlisle you follow the River Eden, (Photo 3), intermittently before leaving it at Crosby on Eden and heading towards Walton then Banks.

Leaving Banks, there is more wall to see as you walk along the road. The route leaves the road as you walk to Birdoswald, passing a good stretch of wall on the way. After Birdoswald, you come to Willowford Bridge, and it was from Bowness to here that the original wall was built of turf rather than stone, as stone was in short supply.

The route is undulating as you continue towards Gilsland and on to Thirlwall. The route passes close by Thirlwall Castle; built in 1300s so it is worth a visit as you are close by. After Thirlwall there is a steep hill to climb as you now come to the best parts of the walk.

Large sections of wall, crags and loughs appear. Once there were quarries, now there are lakes and recreational areas. There are picturesque views of the whole area from the crags and the wall.

It is very undulating in this area as you head towards Cawfields. The crags in the distance mark out your route as you walk up and down the hillsides. Soon you come to Sycamore Gap. This was one of the locations in the making of the film Robin Hood, Prince of Thieves. Crag Lough is ahead, (Photo 8), lying below Highshield Crags. This is a popular view on the route.

After crossing Highshield Crags and passing Crag Lough, the route continues to follow the line of crags over Sewingshields Crags. It is only a comparatively short distance between all the crags, so naturally it is very undulating.

The main fort of Housesteads is directly on your path between the crags. This place is worth visiting, so if you have time to spare, have a walk around the area. The route now heads towards the main B6318 road. It runs parallel with the road for about 6 miles then once you reach Walwick there is a long downhill stretch into Chollerford.

When crossing the bridge at Chollerford there are nice views of the River Tyne. Soon you are walking parallel with the road to Wallhouses then Heddon-on-the-Wall. The Robin Hood pub is on route and Whittledene Reservoir is just past it.

The route from Chollerford often crosses to both sides of the road. There are numerous stiles to cross, which takes some effort at this stage in the walk!

Now you are at Heddon-on-the-Wall where refreshment can be bought. You leave the course of the wall here as it goes through Newcastle. Your path is a long gentle downhill stretch away from the wall to the banks of the Tyne. Passing the golf course, you reach the river, (Photo 11), where a path/cycle track continues all the way to the finish.

Before the finish, there are some very nice views along the riverbank. As you near the city, there are houses not far away at most times. Passing the quayside at Newcastle, there are some very interesting buildings to look at, not to mention the bridges that cross the river, (Photo 12). Take your time and enjoy browsing around the market stalls if open or visit one of the nearby eating-houses.

Following the course of the river on the path/cycle track, you reach a small piece of wall on your left. This is near the finish at Segedunum Roman Fort at Wallsend. Turning left to the finish, go into the main building and museum or even visit the observation tower. This is the end of the walk!

Hadrian's Wall Elevation Chart

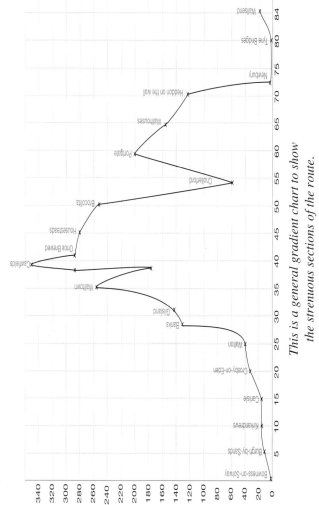

This is a general gradient chart to show the strenuous sections of the route.

Sketch 14

PREPARATION
Planning your journey

Hadrian's Wall Path is an 84 mile trail. To fully appreciate the route and get maximum enjoyment from your walk, you need to walk within your capability.

- Try to walk a shorter distance each day. This allows time to visit monuments and other historical places on route as you pass them.

- Spreading your journey over a longer period enables you to conserve energy.

To enable you to plan your journey I have given two alternative journey times.

4 Day Walk A more demanding schedule, days 3 & 4 being the most demanding.

		Miles/km	
Day	**1** Bowness-on-Solway to Carlisle	15	24.1
	2. Carlisle to Banks	13	20.9
	3. Banks to Chollerford	26	41.8
	4. Chollerford to Wallsend	<u>30</u>	48.3
		<u>84</u>	

6 Day Walk   Allowing time to visit attractions on route.

		Miles/km	
Day	**1.** Bowness-on-Solway to Carlisle	15	24.1
	2. Carlisle to Banks	13	20.9
	3. Banks to Once Brewed	13	20.9
	4. Once Brewed to Chollerford	13	20.9
	5. Chollerford to Heddon-on-the-Wall	15	24.1
	6. Heddon-on-the-Wall to Wallsend	<u>15</u>	24.1
		<u>84</u>	

Daily description for 6-day walk

Day 1 The first day is quite easy, with just a few hillsides to negotiate. It starts with a walk along the shoreline with fine views over the Solway Firth before turning off towards Carlisle. No wall visible around here, but there are many buildings that have used stone from the wall in their construction.

Day 2 Leaving Carlisle you will skirt around the golf course by the River Eden then through the large park area. You pass a folly on your left before crossing the M6 motorway then turning down to the riverside. As you continue, look for parts of the wall as you walk towards Hare Hill then on to Banks.

Day 3 The route now gets progressively more undulating as you reach the central section. Leaving Banks you walk on the road as you pass sections of wall frequently now. Turrets and milecastles (or the remains of them) are to be seen often. You walk down to Birdoswald by a section of wall then on to pass close by Gilsland. The countryside is getting more remote now as you pass the turrets and milecastles on the way to Once Brewed. The picturesque Cawfields and Walltown are not to be missed.

Day 4 This section is the highlight of the journey, with forts like Housesteads to explore and a Roman temple. The scenery is outstanding as you walk the very hilly and undulating path by the wall. Pass a location of the Robin Hood film and enjoy the panoramic views from the crags of the whole area and Crag Lough, (Photo 8). Finally enter Chollerford descending the long straight road to the picturesque village by the river at the bottom.

Day 5 Leaving Chollerford and crossing the River Tyne, you walk parallel with the B6318, as you zig zag to both sides of the road, crossing numerous stiles on route. This section is not too undulating and a nice day walk leading along by the wall to Heddon-on-the-Wall. On route you pass the Robin Hood pub and Whittledene reservoir near Welton.

Day 6 From Heddon-on-the-Wall it is a nice walk, initially descending to the banks of the River Tyne, (Photo 11), then following the flat path/cycleway close by the river to the quayside at Newcastle, (Photo 12). Depending on your timing, you may be able to visit the Sunday market as well as the trendy eating places nearby.

Approaching the finish, still close to the river on the path/cycleway, it is not long before you see the final piece of wall by Segedunum Roman Fort. Visit the viewing tower situated at the finish.

This walk like other long distance walks is considered a challenge. The total distance is 84 miles, so if you are not prepared it could lead to problems. When preparing, consider the following:-

FITNESS   FAMILIARISATION
FOOD   EQUIPMENT

Fitness
The main problem on this walk is the distance and the undulating section covering the central part of the walk. Because of this there is a lot of pressure on the leg muscles, knees and achilles tendon. Exercise should be taken to build up stamina i.e. walking, jogging, cycling and swimming all help to improve fitness.

Walk at a steady pace this will conserve energy and maintain a steady body heat and release of energy. This steady pace will usually help you to overcome steep or difficult sections without becoming exhausted. Some walkers set off at a brisk pace and often become exhausted soon afterwards. The combination of exhaustion and loss of energy can hasten the onset of hypothermia.

Food
Food consumed both before you start and while walking can affect your body heat and energy level. High-energy food such as bananas, rice, pasta, potato and wholemeal bread are all carbohydrate rich and of benefit. A high intake of these carbohydrates coupled with a balanced diet of protein, for building body and muscle strength, should give you the strength and energy to complete this walk.

Familiarisation

Study your map and familiarise yourself with the route and various landmarks, where possible visit the areas before you walk. Note general landmarks and points of interest and make a route plan before you go with times, places, stopping points etc.

Equipment

The equipment you take can mean success or failure, especially if the weather is bad and you have the wrong equipment/clothing. While many people will know what to wear and take, others will not, so this list should help.

Carefully select both personal and safety equipment. Clothing should be capable of keeping you warm and dry and should protect you from the elements.

Boots

Give ankle protection and are an essential item on this walk. A good fitting pair of boots can make the difference between success and failure on any walk. It is appropriate to mention here that toe nails should be cut short before the walk as toes can touch the front of the boots when descending the crags, so doing this should stop you losing your toe nails.

Most types of leather boots will need 'breaking-in' before use. Regular waxing will help keep the leather soft and supple. Before buying boots always try them on wearing the socks you will use with them. The boots should not be too tight as to cramp your toes, likewise not too slack that your feet move around inside.

Socks

These should keep the feet warm and cushion them from any knocks and constant pounding. You can usually buy short, medium or long depending on preference. Whatever your choice they should ideally be approximately 60% wool for good insulating property.

Trousers

Should be loose fitting and ideally made of cotton or a fleece type of material. Cotton trousers will be light to wear, keep you warm and most importantly will dry quickly when wet. Fleece trousers will generally keep you very warm. They are lightweight and can be waterproofed.

Jeans are not suitable for walking as they take a long time to dry when wet and become very heavy. They can also chafe the skin, draw the body heat, so giving you hypothermia, and their insulating property is very low. Do not become one of the jeans and t-shirt brigade.

Hat
Much of the body's heat is lost through the head, so some protection is strongly advised.

Jacket
There is a vast assortment of jackets available for this type of venture from fleece to coated materials that are often breathable. If there is a hood attached this will give good protection around the head.
Most jackets are washable and can be re-waterproofed to withstand the elements for at least a few hours.

Waterproofs/Windproofs
Jackets that are breathable, waterproof and windproof are popular, but whichever jacket you are buying make sure it is waterproof and not just showerproof.

When buying your jacket make allowance for the other items of clothing you would normally wear underneath and indeed extra clothing for cold weather.

Do not wear water/windproofs that are not breathable any longer than necessary as quite often condensation builds up inside. Try to keep the jacket ventilated as much as possible to reduce the condensation.

Breathable Clothing
Generally clothing which is classed as breathable is only breathable as long as the pores of the item are not blocked, e.g. when wet!

Gloves

A pair of fleece, woollen gloves or mittens is strongly recommended. You will find that 5-finger gloves, as opposed to mittens, are probably better, especially in gale force winds when handling map and adjusting compass and clothing.

Rucksack

This should be large enough to hold all your personal and safety equipment described. It should be robust enough to stand the test of putting on and removing in all weathers. It is advisable to put a liner inside to keep items dry in wet conditions.

Emergency Equipment

This includes spare clothing e.g. sweater, socks etc. which should be carried in the rucksack.

Torch

Each person should carry one; take spare batteries and a bulb.

Pencil & Notebook

It may be necessary to take notes on route, especially in an emergency when positions, names, injuries etc. should be written and passed on to emergency services.

Whistle

Each person should carry a plastic whistle (metal ones can freeze in cold) and they should also be familiar with the 'S.O.S.' signal to alert others in times of emergency.

Survival Bag

Usually made of heavy-duty polythene and designed for a walker to get inside to help protect them from the harsh environment and to preserve body heat. It is a piece of safety equipment that may never be used but should always be carried in your rucksack.

THE BODY

RUCKSACK
Containing food, drinks, first aid, and clothing, map and compass.

THE HEAD
Should be kept warm, more heat is lost from the head than anywhere else.

THE BODY
*Should be kept warm.
Build clothes up in layers with wind/waterproofs on top.*

HANDS
Should be kept warm with gloves.

MAIN BODY CORE
Temperature must be maintained.

LEGS
It is important not to wear jeans

ANKLES
Should be protected by wearing boots. These will help stop you going over on your ankle and strengthen it.

FEET
Should be kept well cushioned and dry if possible. Good fitting boots will help prevent blisters

Sketch 15

16

FIRST AID

Knowledge of basic first aid would be helpful on any walk. To be able to bandage cracked ribs, put a sling on or dress a wound can be vital in times of accidents especially on the higher crags, when hypothermia can set in.

In any accident or emergency situation the ability to reassure the casualty and comfort them is very important, do not move the casualty if the accident is of a possible serious nature e.g. a back or head injury. Keep the casualty warm and reassured then send for help. Someone should stay with the injured person. If the injury is not of a serious nature the injured person should, if and when possible, be removed from danger.

The possibility of shock or delayed shock can present further problems for the casualty, so reassurance and company is vital. The majority of accidents happen on the return or second half of the journey, probably due to fatigue, cold, tiredness or complacency. Be aware and alert throughout the walk to possible dangers.

Common Types of Injuries

Cuts and grazes   *Broken Arms/Legs*
Blisters   *Cracked Ribs*
Hypothermia   *Head Injuries*
Sprained Ankle/Wrist   *Gashed Shins*
Toe nails dropping off – cut before you go!

All the above, however minor, can prove fatal, the casualty going into shock, especially on an exposed area of the mountain or in times of panic, fog or adverse conditions, coupled with the injury.

Individual First Aid Kit

Adhesive Dressing   *Waterproof Container*   *Scissors*
Triangular Bandage   *Sterile Dressing*   *Micropore*
Bandage   *Crepe Bandage*   *Sun Cream*
Safety Pins   *Gauze/Lint*   *Insect Repellent*

HYPOTHERMIA

Hypothermia is caused when the body core temperature falls below 35°C. If a walker is not properly prepared for the conditions or the equipment/clothing is not satisfactory then a combination of the cold, wet, exhaustion and the wind chill factor can give a walker hypothermia.

The Signs and Symptoms in Descending Order:-

Shivering
Cold, pale and dry skin
Low body temperature
Irrational behaviour
A gradual slip into unconsciousness
Pulse and respiratory rate slow
Difficulty in detecting breathing and pulse when unconscious
Death

Ways of Preventing Hypothermia

1. Build up body clothing in thin layers, adding on or taking off as necessary.
2. Have suitable wind/waterproofs with you.
3. Take some food/hot drink or boiled sweets, which produce energy and heat during digestion.
4. Wear a balaclava/woolly hat to insulate the head, and some gloves.
5. Shelter out of the wind.
6. Take a survival bag and if conditions dictate, use it.

In any type of emergency/accident situation it is always advisable to come off the higher ground as soon as possible especially in low cloud, snow or other bad conditions. The temperature difference between a valley and the high ground can be several degrees.

Treatment for Hypothermia

1. Provide extra clothing and shelter from the elements.
2. Bodily warmth of others helps in a gradual warming.

3. If well enough come down into a warmer sheltered area.
4. Give hot drinks if conscious.
5. Give chocolate or sweets if the patient can still take food.
6. The casualty should be placed so that the head is slightly lower than the body.

DO NOT *rub the skin or use a hot water bottle as this can cause a surge of blood from the central body core to the surface, this could prove fatal.*

Alcohol should not be consumed on any walk and should not be given to anyone who has hypothermia. The body temperature will be lowered as well as giving a false sense of security.

SAFETY

A route card should be carried by each person and they should all have been involved in planning it.

Details of your route (route plan) should be left with your support team or someone who can monitor your progress and most importantly alert the rescue services if you are overdue. Because you plan a route it does not mean you have to use it. It is better to cancel if there is a problem than to risk lives walking in atrocious conditions or if badly prepared.

Many people do not realise that a calm sunny day in a valley can mean low cloud and gale force winds on high ground like Windshields Crags or Sewingshields Crags, add to this the wind chill factor and a walker badly prepared has got problems. Bad weather can sweep in quickly. It is advisable to listen to the forecast on local radio if possible for the area you are in.

THE WALKERS CODE

The countryside is a place where many people like to escape to and enjoy at various times. To do this we need to look after it when we use it and to preserve it for future generations.

Hadrian's Wall World Heritage Site is a fragile environment. To help protect one of the wonders of the world

- **Be conscious at all times of erosion of the path and try not to walk on the worn grass path, but walk to the side of it.**
- Guard against all risk of fire
- Leave gates as you find them
- Keep dogs on a lead
- Keep to the signed paths
- Protect wildlife, trees and plants
- Take litter home
- Leave nothing but footprints, take nothing but photographs
- Do not walk on the wall or disturb it, and try not to walk alongside the wall when it is wet
- Visit organised paying sites, which are set up to accommodate many visitors
- Do not play radios etc. or create unnecessary noise
- Don't take mountain bikes on the route
- Use public transport whenever you can

NAVIGATION & GRID REFERENCES

The ability to find your way from one place to another especially in bad weather is something that needs to be learned. Although we may have a sixth sense or sense of direction, when the fog closes in even the best of us can get lost quickly.

Before embarking on Hadrian's Wall Walk, you should have an understanding of the basic principles of map reading and compass use. It is not intended that this walking guide should give you the information on how to use navigational equipment but only to point out the need for walkers to be prepared before venturing out especially in bad visibility.

Learning how to read the contours of a map and being able to recognise landmarks seen on the map can be of benefit. Combined with this, basic course plotting and magnetic variation should at least help you get from A to B.

GRID REFERENCES

You may find it necessary at some time to either find a place from a given grid reference or to make a grid reference from a place on a map.

All maps have grid lines running north/south and east/west. These are called 'Eastings' and 'Northings' and these lines have numbers on them. They can be further split into tenths, the numbers range from 00 to 99.

Grid references are normally given in six figures. The first three figures indicate how far to the east the place is. The second three figures indicate how far to the north the place is.

To make a grid reference look from left to right on a map. Read the numbers going from left to right, write the numbers for the grid line to the left of your position, estimate the tenths to your position and write that number down to make 3 numbers.

Now look up your map and write the two numbers from the line just below your position. Repeat the second sequence as above. You should now have six numbers, usually written e.g. G.R. 647556

In using this method you should be able to pinpoint your target or position quite accurately on a 1:25000 scale map. Before you walk Hadrian's Wall, you need to practise until you can both find grid reference points on a map and create a grid reference from a given position.

Over recent years the use of hand help GPS systems has become much more widespread. They are very useful for pinpointing your position, particularly in bad weather. I strongly recommend them. If taking one on this walk, take some spare batteries. See section near back with GPS grid references for this route.

THE ROUTE

Be conscious at all times of erosion of the path and try not to walk on the worn grass path, but walk to the side of it.
KG = Kissing Gate

Take the No.93 bus from Carlisle to Bowness-on-Solway. Exit from the bus by a public house and walk back down the road to a white painted house where a sign for Hadrian's Wall path and 'The Banks' points to the start of the walk.

Your walk starts at a small open shelter close by the beach, G.R. 225628 (Photo 1). A sign points along by the side of houses before turning left onto the road leaving Bowness-on-Solway. Continue on the minor road, which soon runs parallel with the Solway Firth estuary along to Port Carlisle.

At Port Carlisle, you can either take the coast path to the far side of the village or walk directly through the village. Walking along the coast path, you emerge on the road at a bend. A sign states Caravan Park. Cross the road from the beach side and walk along a narrow road away from the beach.

At the entrance to the caravan park, a sign points left along the course of the Vallum. Go through a KG past a farm and continue on the track. Staying on the track for 1km, you come to 'The Highland Laddie Inn' at Glasson, where you turn right, walking past Orchard House.

You see a sign for the path and Drumburgh on the left. Go through a KG into a field and continue along the field keeping the hedge to your right. Go through another two KG together and bear left then through a third KG.

Walk to the far end of the field, keeping the ditch on your left. Go through a metal farm gate where a sign states Hadrian's Wall to left. Walk now on this long straight dusty track G.R. 260593 to Drumburgh. You emerge at a road junction in Drumburgh and turn right, (Photo 2) heading back towards the Solway Firth, which you will soon see. You are now walking on the road by the grassland at the

The start of
the walk at
Bowness-on-Solway

Photo 1

Drumburgh Castle

Photo 2

River Eden
near Kirkandrews

Photo 3

Hadrian's Wall
at Hare Hill

Photo 4

Undulating hillside
near Walltown Crags

Photo 5

Imposing skies
near Windshields
Crags

Photo 6

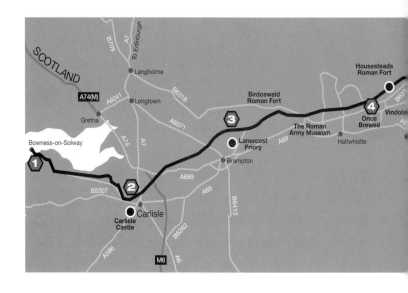

THE ROUTE

1 = Bowness-on-Solway

2 = Carlisle

3 = Banks

4 = Once Brewed

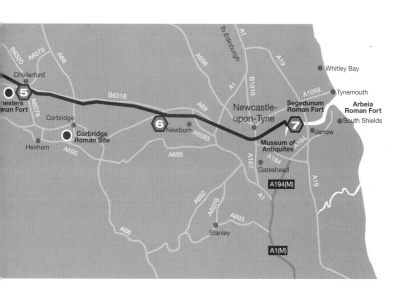

5 = Chollerford

6 = Heddon-on-the-Wall

7 = Segedunum Roman Fort

The 'Trig' point
at Windshields Crags

Photo 7

Crag Lough ahead

Photo 8

Leaving
Housesteads

Photo 9

The Mithraic Temple
by Brocolitia Fort

Photo 10

On the banks
of the Tyne

Photo 11

The modern Quayside
at Newcastle

Photo 12

side of the Solway Firth, heading east on the way to Burgh by Sands.

The village of Boustead Hill is just off to your right as you continue on the long road to Burgh by Sands. Always look for the 'Hadrian's Wall', walk signs. Walk through the village to the far side; pass the church on your right and some white painted houses.

Keep on the left side of road and go through a KG on the left 450m past the church, and follow the path along the edge of the field. Turn right at the top of the field on the course of the wall. This takes you to Beaumont. Go through another KG taking you back onto the road. Walk along the road and look for a sign just before a sharp right hand bend you should see ahead.

Heading towards the houses and into Beaumont village, a sign on the corner points right towards the village green then left at the green, and along the road passing a farm on your left.

On the right is a KG and sign 'Kirkandrews'. Follow that sign to emerge by the side of the river, (Photo 3). Follow the river for a short distance to some houses on your right. Where the path divides, take the higher path leading behind the houses towards Kirkandrews-on-Eden. A little further the path divides again and you bear left down the field 90m from the riverbank. You then walk on a short path and through a KG onto a narrow path between two hedges.

Continue on the path, away from the river to a path junction. Take the left path then immediate right over a concealed stile. Ascend a short banking then go through a farm gate, following a wider track around the edge of a field, keeping the fence on your left. Cross a stile and bear sharp right, crossing another stile. Turn left, walking along the top edge of a field keeping the wire fence just to your left.

Cross a stile into the next large field and descend, keeping the hedge line just to your right. Continue to a gate leading over a stone footbridge at Sourmilk Bridge, G.R. 361581. The path then bears left, keep the hedge line just to your right as you walk up the side of a field towards electricity pylons. Go through a KG by a farm gate and take the narrow path ahead, heading towards the right of a copse.

At the copse you should see a farm and houses at the village of Grimsdale ahead. Head for the farm and go through a KG near a metal gate beside the farm. Now walk on a narrow path taking you by the side of a house into the street. Turn right, passing the entrance to Edenholme Farm and walk to the end of the street. On the corner of the new housing estate look for a KG and sign on your left.

Go through the KG and follow the grass path along the edge of the field, keeping the wire fence just to your left. Go through a gate leading across a footbridge and look for the worn grass path to the right of some trees in the field.

Go through another KG as you approach the river and follow the narrow undulating path up and down steps along the edge of the riverbank and over a footbridge, then ascend a flight of steps. This part of the route is also part of the Cumbria Coastal Way.

Walk through a KG and go alongside electricity pylons, keeping the river just off to your left. Staying close by the river, cross another footbridge and ascend some steps to walk on the stony then grass path into Carlisle. The path stays close by the river as it bends round and under a railway bridge into Carlisle.

Passing a sports field and running track, walk past the changing rooms then look for the footbridge and sign pointing across the River Caldew. On the far side of the river now, you are walking through the park where you soon walk on the main access road through. Pass the sports fields as you head towards the main road and walk under the subway.

On the other side you pass the Riverside Restaurant and bar on your right. Continue on the path close by the river and along by the edge of the golf course. Staying by the river, you pass a school field before coming to the Memorial Bridge where you turn sharp left to cross the River Eden into Rickerby Park. At the far side, take the middle tarmac path through the park.

Walk between the trees to emerge by a cattle grid and sign. Go through a KG, bearing right to go over a footbridge. Pass a tower in a field on your left then on reaching the road, turn towards Rickerby then Linstock Bridge. The road winds round then crosses over the M6 motorway into Linstock. Follow a sign pointing right by some bungalows as you enter the village.

Look for signs further along as you turn left on the minor road. At the end of the lane continue straight along on a small stone track as it winds round and through two farm gates together by a farm then cross the access road there. Continue on the stony track and where it forks, take the left fork. You come to the end of the lane and a sign states Low Crosby, right. Follow this as it takes you to the River Eden.

Walk along the edge of the field by the river as it winds round and onto a small stone track towards some trees with the river on your right and house on your left. You come to a large field. Bear right towards the river where you see a grass track running along the side of the field, parallel with the river. Follow it then you come to a pylon then just past it is a house close by the river and an opening through onto a track by the house G.R. 446593, leading away from the river.

You soon go through a KG into the village of Low Crosby. Walk up Green Lane to the grass roundabout to emerge by The Stag Inn. Turn right at the junction walking past the pub, local school and the church. Continue along the road for 650m towards Crosby-on-Eden. Crosby Lodge is on the right then on the left just before a left hand bend in the road is a path sign and KG.

Go through and along by a fence, through another KG by the farm and continue over a bridge crossing the A689. Go through a KG on the right and follow the track right, around the side of woodland. On reaching a metal farm gate, turn left to walk down Sandy Lane (track). Continue on this grass track as you head towards the Roman Military Way.

The route from Bowness to this point is virtually flat all the way. The track leads on to a narrow minor road where you turn right which is the course of Hadrian's Wall. You come to a farm and continue straight ahead. Look for the path signs and yellow arrows. Stay in same direction along road, grass path and over fields. Pass Bleatarn Farm and tarn on your right side and go through six KG all in same direction. Cross a small footbridge and cross the road at Old Wall and follow the path sign.

Pass the white house at Oldwall, keep right and cross a stile by a gate, still in the same direction. The path leads through a succession of KG. You go through a KG near Whiteflat on a bend at a minor road. Bear left and walk straight down the road where you soon see a sign for Newtown.

Walk through Newtown and at the main road, continue across, looking for a walk sign. Follow the signs by a bungalow right and round by a farm building on a narrow path. You pass Heads Wood on a small hillside on your left then descend some steps, heading towards a farm in the distance on a hillside. Descending from Heads Wood House towards Beck Farm by the side of the field. Keep a hedge on your left following the worn path. Walk round the left side of Beck Farm.

Walk through a KG at the far side of Beck Farm and through several more KG, still in a straight line. Go through Cambeck Hill Farm and through more gates. The path crosses three fields and through a KG into the edge of woodland. Descend some stone steps and cross a footbridge over the weir. Go through a KG then cross a field following a yellow arrow, keeping a line of trees just to your right.

Climb steeply up the short hillside, leaving the farm well off to your left. Go through another KG with a yellow arrow on it, past another farm and cross a cattle grid then turn immediately right through a KG beside the cattle grid. Turn right towards a farm and wood on a stony track and just before the farmhouse, turn left through a KG and go through the wood.

Enter the village of Walton through a KG and onto the main road, turning left. You come to a pub called The Centurion Inn. Continue straight past the front of The Centurion Inn and around a right hand bend to descend the narrow minor road. You come to a white house called Holly Bush Cottage on your left and opposite that is a sign for Hadrian's Wall, which you follow.

Cross the undulating fields on the worn path as you go through another KG following the path signs. Pass Low Wall and follow the path through to a sign pointing right along the edge of the field, keeping the fence line on your right, (Photo 4). You emerge on a minor road where a sign points right down the road.

After approx 75m, a public footpath sign points left to Banks. Turn here through the KG and on a slabbed path for a short distance. Go through a further two KG, following the acorn sign. Continue through more KG and over a footbridge as your path becomes progressively steeper. Go through more KG as your track descends round past a white painted house to emerge on a main road.

Turn left at the main road for approx. 100m then right at the next corner, following the sign down a wooded lane. You pass white painted cottages then at a road junction turn left. Stay on this road for about 3.2km. As you go up a steep hill at the far side of Banks, you see a sign and stile on your right. Cross and continue on a stony path, parallel with the road.

Beside milecastle 51, there is a house beside an old sign to Combcrag and the path descends in front of the house down the lane, keeping just to the right of the wood. A Roman quarry is off on your right in the woods. Approx 90m down the lane, the path turns right through a short piece of woodland. You walk on part of the wall, which is grassed, before your path descends over a stream. You now turn left up a stony unmade track.

You are now on a gradual ascent over fields and through a KG as the route becomes more undulating. Cross steps over a stone wall then turn right following a path parallel with the road. You should see the wall nearby the road. The path emerges on the road further on where you follow a sign for Birdoswald through a KG over a field. There is a visitor centre at Birdoswald.

On route now to Willowford, after leaving Birdoswald, you walk round the remains of turret 48B and bear right, going steeply down a stony track at G.R. 625665 to the bottom then turn left down stone steps to the river. Cross the footbridge over the river then you come to a Roman fort. Soon you cross a cattle grid to emerge by Gilsland School then turn left, walking along the road which descends and bends round through the village.

Pass the Sampson Inn on the main road and as you leave, a road on your right leads to a sign at the far side of a house pointing left along the side of a field. As you near Green Croft Farm, G.R. 645661, cross a ladder stile then continue in front of the farm. Just as you go around the bend on the access track you come to a path sign and a gate. Go through then soon go through another gate.

Follow the path round to the far side of the farm and over a ladder stile then footbridge. Cross a further stile, keeping the boundary wall to your right. Continue towards the next farm keeping the grass-covered wall on your left. Walk parts on the narrow path before descending to a short footbridge and over a ladder stile towards the farm.

Continue towards the road, turning right on the road and as you walk along you see a sign to Thirlwall Castle by a row of cottages. Go through the gate and walk on a grass path by the cottages. (You can continue up to Thirlwall Castle remains then return the short distance again to continue). Turn immediate right over a footbridge, crossing the stream and walking in front of the houses up the stony track.

Cross a stile and ascend the steep hill by the trees. Cross the ladder s tile at the top and continue over the brow of the grass hillside. Emerging on a minor road, turn right to walk along the road to the entrance to the car park by the lake at the National Park recreation site. Walk on a path round the right side of the lake as the path leads up to the cliffs steeply ahead of you, G.R. 672661

Keep the wall on your left as you walk along Walltown Crags on the grass cliff top, keeping away from the edge. Descend to a place know as King Arthur's Well then walk on a slabbed path, over a ladder stile and ascend steeply again up the other side, passing turret 44A. Continue over the crags, (Photo 5), to a strip of woodland. Cross a ladder stile and go through the woodland on a narrow stone path to emerge at the far side.

You come to Aesica Roman Fort just after turret 43A, and a farm on your left. Continue through the ruins and over a ladder stile towards Cawfield Crags 700m ahead. Cross several ladder stiles and pass two farms to emerge at the road at the bottom. Cross stone steps over a wall and the bridge over the stream before turning left. Look for the yellow arrow and the acorn sign as you walk to Cawfield and the lake there, a former quarry.

Walk round the left side of the lake following the path through a KG then ascend through another KG to the side of the wall. Turn left to ascend back to the cliffs, crossing numerous stiles. You descend to cross a minor road at Caw Gap through more KG then ascend steeply up the other side, (Photo 6).

You come to the 'trig' point on the highest point at Windshields Crags near Once Brewed at G.R. 742676 height 345m, (Photo 7). Soon you cross the minor road then a steep ascent up Peel Crags, passing milecastle 39 along the line of cliffs ahead towards Crag Lough (Photo 8). There are a further two small lakes or loughs as they are known off to the left side. Most of the path is grass and soft underfoot as you now walk towards Housesteads, which is the main fort on route.

Descend a short hillside to the left side of Housesteads Fort, (Photo 9), which is worth taking time out to visit as you pass. Leaving Housesteads, go through a gate and follow the public footpath towards Sewing Shields. Go through a KG, keeping the wall on your left now as you ascend towards the trees ahead. There are two steps over a stone wall, which take you into the woods.

Walk through the woods on the winding, ascending path. Cross a ladder stile on leaving and continue ascending over the brow of the hillside on a grass path. Just after milecastle 34 you come to Archers Wood, go through the gate following the path then take a steady descent over fields to arrive at the B6318 road. Follow the course of the wall, parallel with the road for 3600m.

Cross the main road with care, over ladder stiles to Brocolita Military Fort on route. After seeing the temple of Mithraic, (Photo 10), ascend over the hillside on the worn grass path towards the road. Just before the road, bear right in front of the stone wall following the acorn sign and heading for the trees on higher ground. Emerging on the road, cross and follow the sign on the far side, continuing by the remains of the wall.

Cross numerous ladder stiles and fields, keeping parallel with the road up to a wood on higher ground ahead. You pass sections of wall as your path veers off left away from the course of the wall on the descent to Chollerford. Cross several ladder stiles to emerge on a lane. Turn right on the lane and walk the short distance back to the main road then left passing houses and Chesters Roman Fort as you walk into Chollerford.

Walk to the roundabout leading onto the bridge and cross. Just past a fuel garage on your right at the far side, there is a wall sign pointing right. Soon you see a sign to Brunton Turret, follow this back onto the path, (not to the turret). The route follows the main A6079 road.

Walk along the main road on the pavement and go round a left hand bend as you ascend a hill. At the top of the hill is a minor road on the left. Turn left here, signed High Brunton. Just as you get to the main road again you see a path ascending through the wood. Cross a ladder stile and ascend the short steep hillside, still parallel with the road on your left.

You soon walk on another section of wall with a farm ahead, then cross a ladder stile. Cross over the main road at G.R. 930696 and stile then continue parallel with the road again on the left side now. Cross a series of fields over stiles, sometimes on a steep ascent but always parallel with the road. You see St. Oswalds Church off to your left then your path veers off towards the road near a wooden cross.

Walk along the inside edge of the field then go through a KG near St. Oswalds Farm. A tearoom and B&B are nearby.

Walk on a stone slabbed path into next field then you meet an access track to Errington Hill Head Farm. Cross the main road over a stone stile then cross the field, going over a ladder stile into some woodland. You come to a minor road on your right side; go over a ladder stile and continue straight across the road and along the side of the wood, parallel with the road.

Emerging by The Errington Arms pub on the course of the Vallum, at the roundabout, look for a sign on the right at the corner. Walk across by the café and garage then down by the Vallum, still in same direction. Continue down over the fields and over ladder stiles to an impressive entrance to a house and a cattle grid also there. Keep to the right of that then look for the ladder stile in the corner of the field just nearby the road,

Entering the next field continue close by the road towards the trees at the brow of the hill. Cross stone steps in the wall then the path bears off round to the right side of a mound. The path leads back to the road again and over steps into the next field. Cross the road onto the left side just before you get to Carr Hill Farm and walk past a lay-by. Cross to right side then at a minor road, cross onto a good grass track towards milecastle 19.

Ascend some steps then cross the main road and over some stone steps, now walking on the left side parallel with the road. Cross steps over a wall where the path bears diagonally left across the field. Look for a sign and opening in the worn path. The path winds round behind a farm then down by a line of trees at the far side, parallel with the road.

Continue by the line of trees and the course of the wall. Beside turret 18A is a car parking area as you continue by the line of trees close by the road towards a cream painted house. Pass two bungalows at West and East Deanside then bear left at the far side following the public footpath sign to East Wall houses, and going through a gate, then along close by the road again.

Pass a pub called the Robin Hood Inn and turn left at the far side to walk the course of the wall to Whittle Dene Reservoir ahead. At the reservoir, go through two gates to walk between the edge of the reservoir and the road. Ascending from the reservoir you emerge on the road at the top of Harlow Hill beside a farm, turn left to walk in front of the farm buildings on the grass at the side of the road.

Reaching the top of Harlow Hill, stay on the footpath, descending towards Heddon-on-the-Wall. A B&B is at Harlow Hill beside the fuel station. Just past the fuel station, turn off the road and walk on the grass path parallel with the road, descending then ascending in a straight line to the top of Eppies Hill in the far distance. On reaching a track, go through two gates still in same direction.

 Go through a succession of gates as you work your way to the top of Eppies Hill. Ascend some steps then cross the road to walk in the same direction on the other side. The path leads onto the footpath at the side of the road. On reaching Eppies Hill you see a minor road on the right. Follow the sign past a building called Two Hoots (the name is on the corner), then 185m along, turn left to emerge back on the main road again. Continue in same direction as before.

Entering a field by Rudchester Farm, your path bears right round the edge of the field near the farm. Walk down the field keeping the farm buildings on your right, to the minor road, then cross. Your grass path leads towards the A69 main road where you turn left following the ascending path over the A69 on the old road, then back onto your original path.

Follow the path and road along into Heddon-on-the-Wall and on reaching The Three Tuns pub, turn right then first left along Towne Gate. Turn immediately left along Chare Bank, which runs adjacent to the park. The path winds round to a house as you continue down Chare Bank past Garden House. Coming back onto Towne Gate, look for a sign to the right, past the bus shelter then past The Swan pub.

In places your path winds steeply down the minor road, as you head towards the River Tyne. Pass Heddon Banks and further down it bends right, G.R. 132664. Ignore a farm and public footpath on the left. Continue past the trees and the white painted house, now on an unmade road along Close Lea, the road narrows. Look for a sign just below an electricity pylon pointing along an access track. The track ends at Ravens Dene beside a house and is now a narrow path, which runs through a wood and descends steeply.

You emerge on a minor road by some houses and a sign is pointing left along an access road at G.R. 129659. The track winds down and across a golf course. Follow directions to the riverbank. Once at the riverbank, turn left on the path close by the water, (Photo 11), and continue, passing Tyne Rowing Club and The Boathouse pub, beside Newburn Bridge. Cross over the bridge access road, still keeping the Tyne on your right.

The path veers away from the river a little and passes housing estates and factory units. Go under a stone archway and under a small bridge near Leamington Point. Look for signs as you walk through a new housing estate, but generally keeping in line with the river.

Cross a footbridge over a dual carriageway then turn immediately right back towards the river. You emerge on Denton Road and walk down looking for Hadrian's Way sign leading left. Walk to the end of the street and bear right by a metal fence and gates towards a bridge.

Just before the bridge, turn left on a path with bushes and trees on both sides. Continue in same direction to South Benwell roundabout, continue across to traffic lights by Newcastle Audi garage and turn right there down William Armstrong Drive and follow it round past office units then bear right to the river bank again.

Walk past the quayside and modern footbridge in Newcastle still close by the river, (Photo 12). When you see a large white building ahead, your path veers to the left of it, away from the river and over a small metal road bridge spanning an inlet. Just after the bridge, stay in same general direction and work your way along past houses, industrial units and under a railway bridge.

Walk again on a tarmac path/cycle track between the new housing and quayside looking for signs on route. Pass the old Swan Hunter shipyard. A short distance further is the fort and visitor centre marking the end of the wall. A small section of wall is just inside the fence. Bear left just after this to walk up the street to the visitor centre just round the corner.

Congratulations on completing the 84 mile Hadrian's Wall Walk!

POST WALK

After walking Hadrian's Wall, you may like a souvenir to mark the event. The author has produced a selection of Hadrian's Wall souvenirs. These are exclusive to Challenge Publications and include: - certificates for walkers, desk calendars, A4 and A2 colour photographs/posters.

Due to low cloud on high ground or inclement weather, you may not be able to take any photographs. The author has also produced a photograph CD with over 200 superb photographs of the route. This will prepare you for your walk or help you relive your memories. They can be viewed on a PC or on a television via a DVD player. Photographs can be printed from it.

Full details are available **for all souvenirs** and other books by sending for a current price list enclosing a S.A.E. to: -

Brian Smailes
Challenge Publications
7, Earlsmere Drive
Ardsley
Barnsley
South Yorkshire
S71 5HH

To view books on the website, go to **www.chall-pub.co.uk or** to our new National 3 Peaks site **www.national3peaks.co.uk**

USEFUL INFORMATION

Heights of Peaks on route

There are no peaks or mountains as such but the higher ground is principally between Gilsland and Chollerford. At Windshields Crags you reach 345 metres and Hotbanks Crags 325 metres. It is very undulating in that area and its difficulty should not be underestimated.

Nearest Main Towns/Villages on route
Bowness-on-Solway
Burgh by Sands
Carlisle
Walton
Gilsland
Chollerford
Heddon-on-the-Wall
Newburn
Newcastle
Wallsend

Recommended Maps Scale (1:25,000)
Solway Firth - O.S. Explorer No.314
Carlisle - O.S. Explorer No.315
Hexham & Haltwhistle - O.S. Explorer No OL43
Newcastle - O.S. Explorer No 316

Grid References
The grid references below can be put into your GPS to use as a guide to the route.

G.R. 300593	*Coast Path*
G.R. 330591	*Burgh by Sands*
G.R. 340593	*Fields*
G.R. 352590	*Riverbank*
G.R. 355583	*Kirkandrews-on-Eden*
G.R. 370575	*Riverbank*
G.R. 390571	*Riverbank*
G.R. 401565	*Junction of path/A7 road in Carlisle*
G.R. 411564	*River Bridge*
G.R. 420574	*Between Rickerby and Linstock*

G.R. 430584 Near River at Linstock
G.R. 446595 Low Crosby
G.R. 459610 Roman Military Way
G.R. 500628 Newtown
G.R. 512639 Turret 56B
G.R. 561646 Turret 53A
G.R. 615663 Birdoswald
G.R. 649661 Milecastle 47
G.R. 704668 Aesica Roman Fort
G.R. 720668 Cawfield Crags
G.R. 766679 Crag Lough (Photo 8)
G.R. 799698 Turret 35B
G.R. 903705 Walwick
G.R. 919706 Chollerford roundabout
G.R. 980688 Near turret 22B
G.R. 065683 Reservoir
G.R. 122673 Near A69 road
G.R. 133668 Centre of Heddon-on-the-Wall
G.R. 133655 Joining the Tyne riverbank (Photo 11)
G.R. 170651 Leaving the riverbank
G.R. 194647 Crossing under the A1 road
G.R. 205637 Path through Scotswood
G.R. 247634 Newcastle Quayside (Photo 12)
G.R. 293635 Final section
G.R. 301660 Finish at Wallsend

Approximate Walk Times
These timings will vary depending on the skill and fitness of your party but are a rough guide.

Bowness-on-Solway to Drumburgh	= 2 hours
Drumburgh to Burgh by Sands	= 1hr.15 min
Burgh by Sands to Carlisle	= 3hr. 55min
Carlisle to Walton	= 5 hr. 15min
Walton to Gilsland	= 5hr 55min
Gilsland to Thirwall Castle	= 1hr.15min
Thirlwall Castle to Once Brewed (Turret 39B)	= 3hr 15min
Once Brewed to Chollerford	= 6hr 30min

Chollerford to Heddon-on-the-Wall	= 8hr 30min
Heddon-on-the-Wall to Newburn	= 2hr 55min
Newburn to Newcastle quayside	= 2hr 35min
Quayside to finish	= 2hr 25min
	45hr 45min

Baggage Transfer
Walkers Baggage Transfer Co. Ltd
Janet Walker, 3A Townfoot Industrial Estate, Brampton, Cumbria.
CA8 1SW Tel. 0870 990 5549 Fax. 0870 4430135
Email info@walkersbags.co.uk Website www.walkersbags.co.uk
Parties please ring for quote.

Accommodation on route
The following selection of accommodation is not arranged in any order of priority. All are on or within as reasonable distance to the walking route as possible and in route order.
In some places, it was not possible to find B&B's exactly in the villages where you may stop for the night, so the next nearest place is shown where possible.

Bowness-on-Solway – at the start
Wallsend, The Old Rectory. Bowness-on-Solway, Cumbria.
CA7 5AF Tel.016973 51055 Email patsy@wallsend.net
Website www.wallsend.net

Bowness-on-Solway – at the start
Kings Arms, Bowness-on-Solway, CA7 5AF
016973 51426

Stanwix, Carlisle – 0.5 mile from wall
Etterby Country House, Etterby Rd, Stanwix, Carlisle, Cumbria.
CA3 9QS Tel/Fax 01228 510472 Email ffordee@yahoo.co.uk
Website www.etterbycountryhouse.co.uk

Stanwix, Carlisle - 0.1 mile from trail
No.1 Guest House, 1, Etterby St. Stanwix, Carlisle, Cumbria.
CA3 9JB Tel 01228 547285 Email sheila@carlislebandb.co.uk
Website www.carlislebandb.co.uk Pick up available.

Banks – 0.1 mile from trail
South View, Banks, Brampton, Cumbria. CA8 2JH
Tel. 016977 2309 Email sandrahodgson@southviewbanks.f9.co.uk
Website www.southviewbanks.f9.co.uk
Self catering is also available

Grindon – 0.25 miles from wall near milecastle 35
Old Repeater Station, Military Rd, Grindon, Nr. Haydon Bridge,
Northumberland. NE47 6NQ Tel/Fax 01434 688668
Email les.gibson@tiscali.co.uk
Website www.hadrians-wall-bedandbreakfast.co.uk

Greenhead – 0.5 mile from wall
Four Wynds, Longbyre, Greenhead, Cumbria. CA8 7HN
Tel. 0798 4992194 Nigel Jarvis
Email countrymatters@hotmail.com

Twice Brewed – 0.6 miles from the trail
Vallum Lodge, Military Rd, Twice Brewed, Northumberland. NE47
7AN Tel. 01434 344248 Fax. 01434 344488
Email stay@vallum-lodge.co.uk Website www.vallum-lodge.co.uk

Wall – 0.25 miles from the wall, just south of Chollerford
Hadrian Hotel, Wall, Northumberland. NE46 4EE
Tel. 01434 681232 Fax 01434 681512
Email david.lindsay13@btinternet.com
Website www.hadrianhotel.com

Humshaugh – near Chollerford 0.5 miles from the trail
Greencarts Farm, Humshaugh, Hexham. NE46 4BW
Tel. 01434 681320 Email sandra@greencarts.co.uk
Website www.greencarts.co.uk

Heddon-on-the-Wall – On the route
Ironsign Farm, Military Rd, Heddon-on-the-Wall, Newcastle upon
Tyne NE15 0JB Tel. 01661 853802 Email lowen532@aol.com
Website www.ironsign.co.uk

Wylam – 0.1 mile from the trail
Wormald House, Main St. Wylam, Northumberland. NE41 8DN
Tel/Fax 01661 852529 Email jr.craven@tiscali.co.uk
Website www.wormaldhouse.co.uk

Newcastle – 0.5 miles from the trail, 1mile from Tyne bridges.
Clifton House Hotel, 46 Clifton Rd, off Grainger Park Rd, Newcastle Upon Tyne NE4 6XH Tel 0191 2730407 or 2736946
Fax. 0191 2730407 Email cliftonhousehotel@hotmail.com

Campsites
Port Carlisle – outskirts, Camping/Caravan Club site.
Carlisle – Green Acres Caravan Park 2.5 miles from trail
01228 675418
Carlisle – Dandy Dinmont Caravan & Camping Site, Blackford.
01228 674611
Carlisle – West View Camping Site, Grinsdale Bridge, Burgh Rd.
01228 526336 0.5 mile from trail.
Gilsland - The Bridge pub, – camping at the back.
Greenhead – Roam & Rest Caravan & Camping Park,
01397 747213
Haltwhistle – Hadrian's Wall Camping Site 01434 320495
Winshields – Camping Site, Bardon Mill, 01434 344243
Humshaugh – Near Chollerford, Greencarts Farm, Humshaugh,
Hexham. NE46 4BW Tel. 01434 681320 0.5 mile from trail.
Email sandra@greencarts.co.uk Website www.greencarts.co.uk
No sites known near route between Chollerford and Wallsend.

Youth Hostels/Bunkhouses
Banks Head Camping Barn – just past car park in Banks.
Carlisle Youth Hostel – Bridge Lane 0870 7705752 0.25 mile
from trail.
Greenhead Youth Hostel – 0870 7705842   0.5 mile from trail.
Once Brewed Youth Hostel – 01434 344360   0.5 mile from trail
Newcastle Youth Hostel – Jesmond Rd. 0191 2812570 2 miles
from trail.
Birdoswald Youth Hostel – Gilsland 0870 7706124 on the trail.

Public Houses on route, most have food

Kings Arms – Bowness-on-Solway
The Greyhound Inn – Burgh by Sands
Hope & Anchor - Port Carlisle
The Duck Inn – Port Carlisle
Highland Laddie – Glasson
Carlisle - Numerous pubs around the City.
Stag Inn – Low Crosby
The Centurion Inn – Walton
The Samson Inn – Gilsland
The Station Hotel – Gilsland
The Bridge Inn – Gilsland
The Robin Hood Inn – just before Whittledene Reservoirs
The Swan - Heddon-on-the-Wall
The Three Tuns – Heddon-on-the-Wall
The Errington Arms – The Portgate, Junc. of A68.
The Boathouse - Newburn

Main Attractions on route

Birdoswald Fort – Gilsland 016977 47602
Thirlwall Castle - Greenhead
Roman Army Museum – 0.75 mile NE of Greenhead 016977 47485
Cawfields – picnic area on route
Northumberland Nat. Park Centre – Once Brewed 01434 344396
Vindolanda Fort – near Once Brewed 01434 344277
Housesteads Fort – on route 01434 344363
Chesters Fort – 0.5 mile west of Chollerford 01434 681379
Newcastle Quayside - Sunday market, food etc
Segedunum Fort, Buddle St. Wallsend. 0191 2369347

Transport on route

Hadrian's Wall Bus Service is a tourist bus (AD122), which links Bowness-on-Solway and Wallsend. It runs through Hexham, Haltwhistle and Carlisle and stops at the major wall sites. There is limited service at certain times of the year. Local buses do run between the towns and villages on route. Contact Hexham TIC for further details 01434 652220.

Other local buses operate between towns & villages throughout the route. Traveline Tel. No. 0870 6082608

Rail services to
Carlisle are available from all parts of the country. Upon arrival at Carlisle, take the No.93 bus to Bowness-on-Solway to start your walk.
Traveline - all bus and metro services 0870 6082608
National Rail enquiries – 08457 484950
www.nationalrail.co.uk

Tourist Information Centres near route
Carlisle – Old Town Hall, 01288 625600
Brampton – Market Place 01697 73433
Haltwhistle – The Railway Station 01434 322002
Once Brewed – National Park Visitor Centre 01434 344396
Hexham – Wentworth Car Park 01434 652220
Corbridge – Hill Street 01434 632815
Newcastle – 128 Grainger St. 0191 2778000
North Shields – 0191 4546612
General Wall enquiry number – 01434 322002
www.hadrians-wall.org
www.nationaltrail.co.uk

Useful Addresses/Tel No's
Long Distance Walkers Association
Paul Lawrence,
15, Tamarisk Rise,
Wokingham,
Berkshire RG40 1WG
Tel: 01189 790190

This association is set up to further the interests of those who enjoy long distance walking. Members receive a journal three times each year, (strider), which includes information on all aspects of long distance walking.
Website – www.ldwa.org.uk. Email LDP@ldwa.org.uk

Ramblers Association
2nd Floor, Camelford House,
87-90 Albert Embankment,
London SE1 7TW
Tel: 01577 861222

Advice and information on all walking matters. Local groups with regular meetings.

The Countryside Agency for England
www.countryside.gov.uk/access

Heddon-on-the-Wall Heritage Centre
Set within St. Andrews Church, 01661 852696

Birdoswald Roman Fort & Visitor Centre
Open Mar – Nov 10.00 – 5.30pm 016977 47602
Northumberland National Park Centre – Once Brewed
Open Mar – Oct 9.30 – 5.30pm 01434 344396

Housesteads Roman Fort & Museum
Open all year, varied times 01434 344363

Vindolanda Fort & Museum
Varied openings 01434 344396

Chesters Roman Fort & Museum
Open all year, varied times 01434 681379

Arbeia Roman Fort & Museum, South Shields
Varied openings 0191 4561369

Hadrian's Wall Tourism
www.hadrians-wall.org   e mail info@hadrians-wall.org

English Heritage hold various events at places along the wall, particularly through the summer months, for further information of events planned call 0870 3331181 or
www.english-heritage.org.uk/events

The route described in this book was used by the author in 2005 and believed to be correct at the time of publication. Hopefully you have enjoyed your adventure and gained as much pleasure from walking the route as he did. Should you wish to walk other challenging routes, please visit Challenge Publications website at: -

www.chall-pub.co.uk
or the new National 3 Peaks website
www.national3peaks.co.uk

A wide selection of walking guides covering the UK are available including The National 3 Peaks Walk and John O'Groats to Lands End. These books, like the others produced contain everything you need to know to complete the challenge. See list in front of book.

On our website you will find other interesting, and possibly different walks around the British Isles, which are equally as picturesque and enjoyable as this one.

Should you wish to comment on this book or give further information to help keep the book updated then please write to the address below or e-mail via the website. An acknowledgement will be given: -

Please write to: -
Challenge Publications
7, Earlsmere Drive,
Ardsley,
Barnsley.
S71 5HH

GLOSSARY OF WORDS

Bearing - A degree or number of degrees set on a compass; follow the direction of travel arrow walking on that bearing to reach your intended destination.

Centurion – Commander of an infantry.

Cohort – Roman Infantry unit of 500 or 1000 men.

Crag - A steep rugged rock or peak.

Grid Reference - Derived from the national grid reference system. This is used to pinpoint a place on a map by use of letters and numbers.

Kissing Gate - Swing gate that usually lets one person through it at a time by moving the gate backwards and forwards.

Legion – Troops numbering about 5000 men.

Lough – A tarn or lake

Magnetic Bearing - This is a grid bearing taken from a map and the relevant magnetic variation added to it to obtain the magnetic bearing. See the relevant maps for details of current magnetic variation.

Mile (Mille Passus) – a thousand paces which is a Roman mile or 1620 yards.

Path – A walk way or route usually under two metres wide.

Route Card - A plan of action prepared before you leave. A copy to be left with someone so that if you fail to return by a planned time then help can be summoned.

Summit - The highest point of a mountain or hill.

Tarn - A small lake or lough.

Track – A route more than two metres wide.

Trig Point - True name is Triangulation Pillar. These mark the summit of many mountains but not all. It is a small stone pillar with a number on it. The height of the mountain is taken from this point. There are trig points on Windshields Crags, the highest point on the walk, Sewingshields Crags and Limestone Corner.

Turret – A small tower, two between each milecastle.

Notes: